11:36

# What to Say to Get Your Way

What to Say

# to Get Your Way

The Magic Words That Guarantee Better,
More Effective Communication

## JOHN BOSWELL

ST. MARTIN'S PRESS ❧ NEW YORK

www.stmartins.com

Design by Mspace/Maura Fadden Rosenthal

Library of Congress Cataloging-in-Publication Data

Boswell, John, 1945–
    What to say to get your way : verbal swaps for kinder, more
effective communication / John Boswell. — 1st ed.
        p. cm.
    ISBN 978-0-312-58084-1
    1. Persuasion (Psychology)    2.  Interpersonal communication.
I. Title.
    BF637.P4B64 2010
    153.8'52—dc22

                                                2009047035

First Edition: September 2010

10  9  8  7  6  5  4  3  2  1

*To my wife, Carol,*
*my practice partner*

# CONTENTS

# *Introduction* • Words Matter

Imagine the following scenario: You are in a meeting that will finalize a very important negotiation for your company. The situation has become so sensitive that both CEOs are attending. Unfortunately, your principal negotiator is the sales director—let's call him Brad—who is known for his bull-in-a-china-shop "style."

The other company's CEO—let's call him Mr. Smith—says, "We've been back and forth for quite a while now, and I think we've been more than fair in considering all of your proposals—"

"I totally disagree," Brad interrupts. "Just yesterday I was completely stonewalled by your marketing director."

Immediately the room grows very tense. Since you've been privy to most of the negotiations, you decide you'd better say something before the roof blows. "Mr. Smith," you say, "we'd argue that we have not yet been able to get all of our ideas out on the table . . ."

Everyone relaxes a bit and Mr. Smith continues, "In any event, the offer we are passing around is our final offer. At this stage it's take it or leave it. We don't want to discuss this any further. We don't want to get into a bidding war. If you have a better offer, then you should take it."

Before anyone else can open his mouth, Brad jumps in. "You know how much we want to do this deal with you, Mr. Smith, but really we aren't even in the same ballpark. You'll have to come up with at least another $1 million." Brad goes on for another two minutes, though it seems like twenty, about what a great deal this is, here are all the benefits, blah blah blah—completely oblivious to the atmosphere in the room.

When he finally shuts up, everyone is staring down at the table . . . except for the two CEOs, who are staring daggers at Brad. In a last-gasp effort you say, "I guess what Brad is asking is whether there is any wiggle room here at all? Are you at all negotiable? Can we have a few days to at least sweeten our package of benefits? That's a no-lose for you."

Mr. Smith reluctantly agrees, and as people get up to leave, Brad is now staring daggers at you. But your CEO gives you a quick wink and nod before walking out of the room.

Damon Runyon once said that "all life is 5–4 against." Fortunately, as I hope this story illustrates, with the slightest change of tone or inflection, or, more concretely, with a savvy turn of phrase, you can change the odds to your favor.

This is a book about being an effective communicator by using the tricks of the trade, whether your trade is that of a psychiatrist, a politician, or a diplomat. Since I am none of these, why is this subject still of particular interest to me? First, in speaking to other members of the human race, we all pretty much want the same thing— to be understood (therapists call it "having a voice"). But we all seem quite adept at getting in our own way. We want to say "I think . . ." or "I believe . . ." or "I feel . . . ," but instead out comes "You are . . ." or "Your problem is . . ." or "You know what's wrong with you . . . ?" End of communication. End of conversation.

You can know everything there is to know about body language, the games people play, and emotional intelligence, but at the end of the day being understood mostly comes down to the actual words that come out of your actual mouth. In the interest of kinder, better communication, let us examine the words that inflame and the words that can take their place.

Ironically, it's hard to find a book on effective communication that effectively communicates. Most books in the self-help or business genres (which is where I also see this fitting because not alienating people is good business)—particularly the "Six Laws . . . ," "Seven Steps . . . ," and "Eight Rules . . ." types of books—generally follow the same pattern: The introduction or the first chapter summarizes the entire book, and the other chapters tell you more about each point or step or rule than you could ever care to know. My attempt is to do just the opposite— to cram a hundred-thousand-word book on communication skills into fewer than a few thousand words.

Here's how the book is organized. After the first two chapters, each of the remaining chapters offers a simple communications precept, such as "Avoid confrontation" or "Don't be annoying," followed by specific examples of what *not* to say and what you might want to say instead.

Becoming a better and more effective communicator is a process, and the process is one of becoming more self-aware—of knowing how you're coming across in any situation, whether it's personal or professional, whether it's an intimate moment, a business meeting, or a speech to a thousand people. It is my hope that this book will help you to develop this self-awareness.

# You've Got the Power!

RECENTLY, WHILE ON JURY DUTY, I was sitting in the waiting room reading my *New York Times* when a very large—okay, fat—woman tried to squeeze by me. She was carrying a big, heavy bag and, as she stepped over me, she hit me in the head with it.

I was about to say something, but she sat down and glared at me as though that was exactly what she was hoping for. Discretion being the better part of federal courthouse valor, I decided to say nothing and went back to reading my paper.

A few minutes later she got up to go hand in her jury notice. As she headed back to her seat, I was ready for her; I had scooted my seat back about a foot. But as she passed by, she hit me in the head with her big, heavy bag again.

There was one empty seat between us where I'd been

keeping my unread sections of the paper. But this time, as she glared at me, she also plopped her bag down right on top of my newspapers.

Now I felt I had to say something, but the words that came out of my mouth were so far out of left field it was as though they were coming out of some other person.

What I said was, "You're welcome to read my paper if you'd like."

For a moment a confused look crossed her face, as if she didn't know what to say next. Once she collected herself, however, and after a couple of false starts, she smiled and said, "Thank you. That's very nice." Then she picked up The Arts section and began to read.

What power! Just like that I had taken a potentially inflammatory situation and poured water on it, turning it to my advantage in the process. But what was even more significant, I believe, is what I didn't say, which could have been anything from "Excuse me, your bag is on my newspapers" to "Get your goddamn bag off my papers, bitch," which, given the venue, might have ended up getting us both thrown in jail.

Why "You're welcome to read my paper" came out of my mouth instead, I really don't know, although several years ago—in an effort to curb my it's-all-about-me approach to life—I came up with a number of rules for myself (such as saying hello and nodding to fellow passengers when they got on "my" elevator and slowed me down). In the same vein, I have two major rules for riding in a cab: Don't tell the cabdriver how to go and don't tell the cabdriver where to go (not as in a destination but as in "to hell"). Instead, upon exiting, I force myself to say something nice like, "Thanks for the ride" or "Have a good day."

The thing about these two rules is they have absolutely nothing to do with the cabdriver and everything to do with me. Opting for patience over my temper just makes me . . . feel better. For a moment, and only very slightly, it brightens my day and gives me a sense of control, no matter how false or fleeting that control actually is.

Any way you slice it, words do matter, and the words you choose matter a lot. And words not only matter, words hurt. (The single greatest disinformation campaign of childhood is the "sticks and stones" rhyme.) They are like barbed arrows, which, once beneath the skin, not only begin to fester but are difficult to take out and often leave a lasting scar.

Once the wrong words come out of your mouth, not only can't you put them back in, they almost invariably provoke an even more hostile response. A war of words is like violating a nuclear nonproliferation pact: "If you bomb me, I'm going to bomb you back twice as hard."

Sometimes saying the right thing is just a matter of being nice. About ten years ago two women self-published a book called *Random Acts of Kindness*, which went on to become a bestseller. Around the same time, a novel by Katherine Ryan Hyde titled *Pay It Forward* also became a bestseller and was subsequently made into a movie. Together they formed what became known as the kindness movement, with its essential karmic message being: What goes around, comes around, but even if it doesn't—kindness is its own reward.

Since we all sort of know this anyway, then why is being nice, not saying the wrong thing, and saying the right thing in its place so hard? Because we are human. And because we are human we don't always think before we act. And because we are human we have feelings. And because we have feelings, our feelings can get hurt. And when our feelings get hurt (the whole fight-or-flight thing), we lash out.

The problem is compounded by the fact that lashing out can be very intoxicating: "Boy, I put him in his place," "That'll teach 'em," "Now she knows who's boss." But that kind of high is usually short-lived, followed by an emotional low or just plain feeling bad.

So how can we help ourselves say the right thing before the wrong thing comes out of our mouths? Well, one thing we can do is try to develop a more conscious awareness of how our words and actions affect others.

Good luck with that! Unfortunately most of us, including me, don't walk around with this kind of self-awareness even when we try. Worse, when this kind of awareness does occur to us, it's usually after the fact.

I believe, however, that by following a few simple guidelines and some specific examples, both of which this book offers, we can train ourselves to say the right thing most of the time.

We should also be well motivated. What this book is really about is getting ourselves heard by not arousing the listener's hostility while using different words to say basically the same thing. It is essentially about not being our own worst enemy, about getting out of our own way.

Another thing you might want to think about is memorizing some of the phrases in this book. That's not as daunting or as irritating as it may sound. There are only a finite number of phrases that get you the results you want. Simply flip through this book and see if anything strikes a chord. If so, then maybe this book could be helpful.

Back to my jury duty story. Did I really have any power over that woman? I think the answer is yes. By saying the right thing to control the situation, I controlled her, and by controlling her I controlled the outcome. In fact, we had a nice nodding relationship over the remainder of the two days. When they finally dismissed us at the end of the second day, our paths crossed once again and I had the opportunity to tell her what I was really thinking:

"Have a good day."

# Six Degrees of Conversation

IF THE WHOLE IDEA IS to get yourself heard, then it's not just what you say, it's also how you say it. Your tone, your inflection, your body language—all adding up to the way you come across—can make all the difference in the world.

My most frequent conversational transgression is using a tone of voice that sounds like a combination of annoyance and contempt. I call this tone of voice "the implied idiot," meaning I don't have to actually say a parenthetical "you idiot" at the end of a statement for the listener to get my drift, as in, "Why would they possibly agree to that (you idiot)." It can be a conversation ender, but more often it just pumps up the volume.

In addition to the strategies and examples proposed in the following chapters, here are six suggestions for keeping your conversational "attitude" at a minimum and dramatically improving your chances of getting yourself heard.

1 • **Think ahead** (before the words jump out of your mouth).

2 • **Listen more** (thereby talking less).

3 • **Pay attention** (actually hear what someone has to say).

4 • **Listen empathetically** ("I'm hearing you").

5 • **Slow down** (if you speak too fast).

6 • **Lower your voice** (if you really want to be heard, whisper).

# A Short Letter of Agreement

There are times when you would like the protection of a contract but the matter is too small (or not worth the expense to take to a lawyer). You must consider the old bromide "He who represents himself has a fool for a client," and since I'm not a lawyer myself I will not attest to the ironclad validity of what is written below. But if the point is to get something on paper, then I suggest the following format.

Dear _____,                                          Date

The purpose of this letter is to confirm the understanding that has been reached between [his name] and myself, [your name], with respect to _____. Our understanding is set forth below.

1. [Name] agrees . . .
2. [Name] agrees . . .

[as many numbered paragraphs as you need]

Please sign and date both copies of this letter, which will then constitute a binding agreement between us. Please return one countersigned copy to me.

Thank you.

Sincerely,
[your signature]

_____Date:_____

[his name]

# Use "I"
# (Put It on You)

It may seem odd to suggest starting a sentence with the vertical pronoun, otherwise known as "I," without having it sound egotistical. Indeed, it can be when attached to certain verbs, such as "I am" or "I did."

But when attached to certain other verbs, like "I feel" or "I think" (as opposed to "you are" or "you do"), it has the reverse effect by putting the burden of responsibility on you. Not only does it eliminate the aggressive accusatory tone, but no one can take offense with how you personally feel or how you personally think.

What follows are a few examples—both the wrong way and the right way—of taking it off them and putting it on you.

*Don't Say:*

"You are . . ."

"You do . . ."

"You don't . . ."

*Don't Say:*

"Don't play games with me."

*Say:*

"I think you're playing games."

*Don't Say:*

**"That's not fair."**

*Say:*

"I don't think you're being fair."

*Don't Say:*

"Pay attention."

*Say:*

"I'm not reaching you."

Don't Say:

"You don't get it."

Say:

"I'm not making myself clear."

**Don't Say:**

"What you said was ..."

**Say:**

"What I heard you say was ..."

Don't Say:

"You're just using me."

Say:

"I'm feeling used."

Don't Say:

"You never listen to me."

Say:

"I feel like I'm not being heard."

Don't Say:

"You're missing the point."

Say:

"I may be missing the point."

*Don't Say:*

**"You screwed up."**

# Applying for a Job/
# Cover Letter

Enough books have been written on how to write a résumé to fill an entire library. What is often underplayed, however, is the importance of the cover letter or cover e-mail. If the job has attracted a lot of résumés, it is not an exaggeration to suggest that 80 percent of the applicants will be eliminated just from the letter alone. In fact, the main purpose of a cover letter is to keep from eliminating yourself.

If there is one place where spelling/punctuation count it is the cover letter/résumé. One typo can be an excuse to throw out the whole package.

When it comes to what you *should* include in your letter, remember this: Whoever's reading your résumé probably has more in common with you than you think. Just like you, your boss-to-be hates when his or her time is wasted, loves to be flattered, and appreciates a warm, kind, and humble tone from a potential employee.

Understanding your potential employer's psyche is the first step toward your perfect cover letter. To show that you don't intend to waste anyone's time, keep your letter brief and prove you've carefully read the job posting. This means parroting back the job title and requirements in a creative and thoughtful way (so your new boss can be sure you're not a robot-drone).

Next, do your homework and use what you've learned to dish out a compliment. Does your potential company have a Web site or product? Find something specific about the company/product/mission statement that intrigues you and, in one sentence, convey your enthusiasm to your potential boss.

And finally, if the job calls for it, show some personality. A job opening in the FBI doesn't merit a joke-riddled cover letter, but a job in the arts may deserve a humorous line or a remarkable turn of phrase. Don't be afraid to make your résumé stand out if you're applying to a position where your personality will be one of the most important items on your skill-set list.

# E-mails

Most people agree that there are way too many e-mails out there. Respond only to e-mails that demand a response and consider everything else informational.

The biggest problem with e-mails is that they are too easy to send and, as an unintended result, often come across as harsh or curt. If you can afford the time, write the e-mail, then come back later and reread it, and only then hit Send. At the very least, review it carefully not just for mistakes but also for tone.

Always address an e-mail to the person by name and always close by including your own name.

Always include a subject. The subject line can be a chance to draw attention to an e-mail, particularly if it is lighthearted or humorous. If, for instance, you are asking someone out for lunch, the subject can be "Lunch" or something like "Big Opportunity."

# Put It on "Them"

Not always, but on occasion, it's wise to make clear that you must defer a decision to a higher power (like your boss, not God). Say a lazy but dear friend is trying to get hired at your company and asked you to pass along his résumé. Now he wants to know why he hasn't gotten an interview. It's better to admit your place in these matters. "Unfortunately, I have no influence with HR" will save your friendship, whereas expressing your personal opinion ("Actually, Hal, you're too dumb and lazy for that job") is a relationship ender. Use this tactic only if it's true that another party—"them"—not you, is *actually* better suited to deal with the question or request.

Every once in a while you'll also come across the opportunity to place blame on nothing (or the unruly whims of Fate, if you prefer). When the rare chance comes up, think about using one of the following phrases.

*Don't Say:*

"I won't show you that."

*Say:*

"I'm not allowed to show you that."

*Don't Say:*

**"That's your problem."**

*Say:*

"It's out of my hands."

"It's not my decision to make."

Don't Say:

"Stop trying to control this."

Say:

"This is something you can't control."

Don't Say:

"Here's how you need to do it."

Say:

"This is how I was told to do it."

Don't Say:

"I can't help you."

Say:

"There's nothing I can do."

**Don't Say:**

"Look what you've made me do."

**Say:**

"Look what's happened."

# Please

"Please" is generally considered a polite way to ask for something. But it can also be used in a way to take the hard edge off of your response to someone who is provoking you.

For instance, if you say, "Don't order me around" or "Stop ordering me around" to someone, even if she in fact is ordering you around, it puts her on the defensive and she is likely to come back with a denial—"I'm not ordering you around"—which just invites a new argument ("Yes, you are." "No, I'm not.").

However, just by putting "please" in front of the same statement ("Please don't order me around"), even if you get the same response, the defensive posture has been exorcised ("I'm not ordering you around, but what I'm trying to say is . . .").

Interestingly, it doesn't work the same way for the "magic words" "thank you." If, for instance, you say to someone, "Thank you for not smoking," you might get punched in the mouth. On the other hand, if you say, "Please don't smoke," she may still not like it, but you are probably going to get compliance.

# 5

# Can/Could & May/Might

REMEMBER THE OLD SALES TECHNIQUE: Make them think it was *their* idea. Well, changing a demand or accusation to a "can/could" or "may/might" question is kind of like that: It offers a choice to the person you're conversing with, while gracefully imposing your preference on him.

By adding "can/could/may/might" to a sentence, you appear less forceful and more open to a conversation. This technique also ensures that you don't put the person you're conversing with on the defensive, which will make you more likely to get what you want in the end.

Don't Say:

"That's a terrible idea."

Say:

"Can I talk you out of it?"

Don't Say:

"You need to . . ."

"You must . . ."

*Say:*

"You might . . ."

"You could . . ."

Don't Say:

"You made a mistake."

Say:

"Could you have made a mistake?"

Don't Say:

"That's the wrong way to do it."

Say:

"You might want to try doing it this way."

Don't Say:

"You're not helping."

Say:

"Could you help me?"

**Don't Say:**

"Slow down."

**Say:**

"Can you speak more slowly?"

Don't Say:

"Relax."

Say:

"You might be overreacting."

*Don't Say:*

"Here's what you need to do."

*Say:*

"Can I make a suggestion?"

*Don't Say:*

**"Don't talk to me like that."**

*Say:*

"Could you say that again?"

*Don't Say:*

**"Don't tell me what to do."**

*Say:*

"Can I decide for myself?"

*Don't Say:*

"I don't need this."

"I don't have to put up with this."

"I don't have to take this."

Say:

"Could you be more respectful?"

# Giving Advice

Giving advice is tricky. Even if someone is asking for your advice, it doesn't necessarily mean he wants it. Oftentimes, he is just looking for support or for you to confirm or at least acknowledge a course of action on which he has already decided.

As a general rule, don't give advice unless it is asked for, but if you do, first acknowledge in some way that it is unsolicited, such as, "Not that you've asked for my advice, but . . ."

Don't generalize. Try to keep it to the topic at hand and on solving the problem, and above all else don't use your advice as an opportunity for commenting about the person who has solicited it.

Start out with something like, "I'm not one to give advice but . . ." or "What you might want to consider is . . ." Focus only on the solution. If, for instance, the issue is punctuality, you could say, "You might want to consider setting your watch a few minutes fast, or making it a point, rather than arriving on time, to get there five minutes early."

# Accepting a Job

The key to accepting a job, whether over the phone, in writing, or in person, is to keep it direct, short, and sweet. Words like "delighted," "pleased," even "thrilled" are good, but avoid any phrase, such as "You won't regret it," that would give someone any reason for pause. It should go something like this:

"Thanks very much for offering me a position as _____. I'm delighted and I accept. The terms we discussed are fine and I look forward to starting at your earliest convenience. I'm excited to be part of..."

If there are conditional or extenuating circumstances, state them as directly and as succinctly as possible:

"As you know, the salary you have offered is less than what I need in order to make ends meet. Are you at all open to further discussion?"

"I feel it is appropriate to give my current employer a minimum of two weeks' notice and I will be able to start immediately after that."

# Avoid Confrontation

Essentially, this entire book is about avoiding confrontation. However, during tense moments we often reach for provocative clichés that escalate a heated conversation to a full-fledged argument. The following pages contain some phrases that are tempting to use (because they do it in the movies) but aren't actually as effective as their less glamorous, less dramatic alternatives.

*Don't Say:*

"You're scatterbrained."

*Say:*

"You made an error."

Don't Say:

"Don't you dare."

Say:

"Please don't."

"That's a lie."

Say:

"That's not true."

"Are you sure?"

Don't Say:

"Get out of my face."

Say:

"Please give me some space."

*Don't Say:*

"I can't believe you said that."

*Say:*

"I'm surprised by your reaction."

*Don't Say:*

"What do you think you are doing?"

*Say:*

"What are you trying to do?"

*Don't Say:*

"Mind your own business."

"It's none of your business."

*Say:*

"It's personal."

*Say:*

"Let me rephrase that."

"We're not on the same page."

Don't Say:

"You're wrong."

Say:

"I would argue that . . ."

"I'd make the case that . . ."

Don't Say:

"How could you do this to me?"

Say:

"You really hurt my feelings."

Don't Say:

"That's your fault."

Say:

"I should have explained."

Don't Say:

"You're full of it."

Say:

"We're both full of it."

# Acknowledging Receipt

The purpose of an acknowledgment of receipt, whether it is a package or an e-mail or an invitation, is to confirm whatever was sent has been received and what actions it will trigger.

"This is to confirm that we have received your letter regarding _____. I must share it with several of my colleagues, so please give me a couple of weeks to get back to you."

"Thanks very much for the invitation to _____. I will definitely see you on _____. I'm looking forward to the_____."

# How to Fire Someone

Whether firing for cause or because the company is experiencing difficulties, most people feel bad about having to let someone go. It is also difficult because exposing your regret in any way makes it harder on the person being fired.

Any ambivalence at all comes across as giving someone false hope.

It is best to keep your firing speech, if not sweet, at least short. Be direct and don't equivocate. Use the word "terminate." Explain the company's severance policy, if any. Volunteer to write a reference letter if you feel comfortable doing so.

Say something like this: "I've got some bad news. Your job here has been terminated. We have a severance policy that Human Resources will explain to you." Or, if the company is small, "I'm going to give you two weeks of severance pay. I can also give you a reference letter. I'm sorry, but the decision is final."

# 7

# Make It a Question

An accusation doesn't have an automatic response, except possibly tears and/or yelling. On the other hand, turning your accusation into a question is less threatening *and* it requires that the other person give an answer, which is much better than inciting him to devolve into an angry and emotional mess. You don't need to point fingers to make a point. Try a question instead; you may be surprised that the person on the other side of the conversation has a good answer.

*Don't Say:*

"I don't have time for this."

*Say:*

"Can you give me some more time?"

Don't Say:

"I don't get it."

Say:

"Would you mind explaining that?"

Don't Say:

"Don't interrupt me."

"Quit cutting me off."

Say:

"May I finish?"

Don't Say:

"You're acting so mean."

Say:

"Why are you acting so mean?"

*Don't Say:*

"You owe me an apology."

*Say:*

"Don't you think you should apologize?"

*Don't Say:*

**"Don't give me that dirty look."**

*Say:*

"Why are you looking at me like that?"

*Don't Say:*

**"Don't raise your voice."**

*Say:*

"Are you yelling at me?"

## Don't Say:

"I don't see the point of this."

## Say:

"What are you looking to
get accomplished here?"

# Give Them Back
# Their Own Question

People, particularly passive-aggressive types, especially in the workplace, often ask a question not because they want an answer but because they want to express their displeasure. It's called having an attitude.

For instance, if someone says, "Why wasn't I invited to that meeting?" he probably isn't really interested in knowing why he wasn't invited. He is interested in letting you know you owe him an explanation and it'd better be good.

The way to defuse this kind of verbal stink bomb is to give his question right back to him. In other words, the answer to why he wasn't invited to that meeting is, "Did you want to be invited to that meeting?"

Now he has no place to go with it other than to express what he should have expressed in the first place: "I should have been invited because . . ." He's not going to get to have his fight.

# Offer the Solution

Nobody wants to be known as a whiner. Spouting your problems makes you seem helpless, but there is a way of expressing concern without being a complainer: Make the solution part of your expression of distress. If you are feeling lonely, say that you could use someone to talk to rather than complaining about spending too much time alone. At work, tell your boss you'd like some extra help or time on a project rather than saying it's too difficult and you don't have time for it. Bad news is always easier to take if a solution is in the mix.

The same is true for criticism. Listing someone's faults isn't nearly as productive as telling a person what he or she *could* be doing right. Be specific. Instead of saying, "I wish you weren't so self-centered," you could say, "I wish you would help me out sometimes." Offering a concrete way of fixing the problem makes you look like a savior, even if someone else has to do all the legwork.

# Don't Be Annoying

AN ANNOYING PERSON PRETENDS TO empathize when he clearly can't. An annoying person pretends he's made a huge sacrifice when he clearly hasn't. An annoying person simplifies complex situations and complicates simple situations. Don't be an annoying person.

Instead of false empathy, express sympathy. Don't use clichés just because they're common phrases—say what you really mean. Don't put contingencies on your words: "I'm sorry" and a "but" should never be in the same sentence. Saving your "but" for later may also save you a black eye.

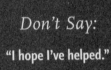

Don't Say:

"I hope I've helped."

Say:

"I'm sorry I can't be more helpful."

**Don't Say:**

"I feel your pain."

**Say:**

"I can't imagine how you must feel."

Don't Say:

"I'm sorry you feel that way."

"I'm sorry you were offended."

"I'm sorry but . . ."

Don't Say:

"I'm doing this for you."

Say:

"I'm trying to help."

*Don't Say:*

"It's take it or leave it."

*Say:*

"That's the best I can do."

# Asking for a Raise

Receiving a raise is often about timing—the company is doing well or you are doing well in a way that can be documented, such as a positive performance review or a big deal you have just finalized.

You deserve a raise either because you can prove your positive contribution or, in terms of your skills or responsibilities, your value to the company has increased. You don't deserve a raise because somebody else is making more than you or because your rent just went up.

The biggest X factor in a raise is your relationship with your boss. If it's bad, you probably aren't going to get a raise; if it's good, enlist his or her help by saying something like this:

"As you know, I love my job and I love working here. However, I have a problem and I am hoping you might be able to help. I've been here for a little over a year now and during that time [state what you've done for the company, emphasizing any increased responsibilities]. I think a salary increase of [state number] is justified and would more accurately reflect my current contribution to the company."

# Avoid the Negative

IT'S EASY TO TURN EVEN a compliment into a negative comment if you use "no," "not," or any other words relating to deficiency and failure. For example, if your boss said to you, "Keep up the good work. That report wasn't as bad as the last one," it wouldn't exactly fill you with joy. But if she said, "Keep up the good work. Your report was well done," you'd feel great about yourself.

Others will want to be around you if you make a point of using positives rather than negatives wherever possible. And when you do decide to go into negative territory, your words will have extra bite.

*Don't Say:*

"Do your own dirty work."

*Say:*

"I don't feel comfortable doing that."

*Don't Say:*

"That's not the way it is."

*Say:*

"I take a different view."

Don't Say:

"That's not what I said."

Say:

"Let me explain that again."

# Writing a Thank-You Note

There are a lot of things you can do to stay in the good graces of your contacts, but none of them will matter if the people in your life don't feel appreciated. From your workplace to your family and friends, no one wants to feel as if his or her act of generosity has gone unnoticed. As such, the thank-you note isn't just a nicety, it's a necessity.

Luckily, a good thank-you note is simple: You need only include a few lines thanking someone for whatever, specifically, she's given you; add a sentence about how you've used or appreciated the item, idea, etc.; and write a final sentence of general well-wishing or an expression of desire to see the person again, such as, "Let's get together soon."

Don't write a memoir; there's no need to wander from the act of generosity you're writing about. It is important to personalize your letter, but it's also important to be succinct and timely. For example:

Dear George and Darlene,

Thank you so much for the Bed Bath & Beyond gift card. I used it to buy new springform pans so I can improve my baking!

I know you two have a lot going on, and I really appreciate your thinking of me on my birthday. I'd love to have you over sometime soon for a taste of my new and improved strawberry cheesecake.

Take care, and thanks again for your thoughtfulness!

Sincerely,

Trish

# Soften the Message

CONTRARY TO THE BELIEF OF the impolite masses, one does not need to choose the harshest and loudest language available to be heard. In fact, most people are impressed by tact (that's the whole reason tact exists in the first place). Assuming constructive conversation—not making someone feel bad or angry—is your goal, it is in your best interest to think of what you want to say ("Go jump in the lake, you middle-management moron") and then take the bite out ("I'm not sure we're suited to work together").

Even a middle-management moron will get the hint.

*Don't Say:*

"I don't want to talk about it."

*Say:*

"I'd rather not discuss it."

*Don't Say:*

"That's no excuse."

*Say:*

"That's not acceptable."

Don't Say:

"I disagree."

Say:

"I'm not sure I'd agree that . . ."

Don't Say:

"That's not fair."

Say:

"I'm surprised."

Don't Say:

"What was I supposed to do?"

Say:

"How would you suggest I handle it?"

Don't Say:

"Here's what I expect . . ."

"What did you expect?"

*Say:*

"Here's what I was hoping . . ."

"What were you hoping?"

*Don't Say:*

**"Let me make myself clear."**

*Say:*

"I hope I've made myself clear."

Don't Say:

"Stop freaking out!"

Say:

"Let me give you a moment to de-stress."

**Don't Say:**

"That's not what I said."

**Say:**

"Let me explain that another way."

# Between You and Me

This is not a grammar book, nor is it intended to be. Yet the one grammatical usage that drives people who know better up the wall is the use of the subjective case—"I," "we," "he," "she," and "they"—with the preposition "between."

A preposition always takes the objective case. That means "between you and I" is always wrong, as is "between he and I," "between he and she," "between you and they," and "between you and he."

What is always right is "between you and me," "between him and me," "between him and her," "between you and them," and "between you and him."

What is particularly annoying about this grammatical error is that the people who make it tend to make it a lot, as though they want to sound more correct or erudite when they are in fact just plain wrong.

For some reason it is very uncomfortable to correct people who make this particular mistake, which is why I've included it here. Give them a copy of this book and let them discover it for themselves.

# Opening Softeners

Often the first phrase or sentence out of your mouth sets the tone for everything that follows. There are any number of opening phrases that can help soften almost anything you are about to say afterward:

"I could be mistaken but . . ."

"To my way of thinking . . ."

"As I understand it . . ."

"It seems to me that . . ."

"You might want to consider . . ."

"I'm sure you thought of this but . . ."

"To the best of my knowledge . . ."

"I wonder if . . ."

# Be Polite

SOME WORDS IMPLY INSULT, and I dealt with those in previous chapters. But sometimes words that don't have offensive connotations at all simply have an alternative that sounds more polite. Opting for your most well-mannered choice will add value to your message. People's ears are more likely to perk up when they hear an opinion given by someone who handles his or her language and audience with unusual care.

Don't Say:

"Don't be so rude."

Say:

"Could you be a little more polite?"

*Don't Say:*

"You really pissed me off."

*Say:*

"You've really upset me."

**Don't Say:**

"I have to go to the bathroom."

"I have to pee."

**Say:**

"I have to step out."

# I'm Sorry

When spoken together, "I'm sorry" may be the hardest words to say in the English language, yet there are no words that have more magic. As soon as "I apologize" or "I'm sorry" comes out of your mouth, you can literally feel the heat go out of the exchange or the self-righteousness out of the argument.

However, just because they're effective words doesn't make them easier to say. The key is that it is very rare that an argument is 100 percent one-sided, so what you need to do is clean up your side of the street even if it's only 10 percent or even 1 percent of the mess. "I'm sorry for my part" or "I apologize for my part" is just so much easier to say and it costs you nothing.

# Office Etiquette

A PROFESSIONAL SETTING REQUIRES YOU to conduct yourself more formally and neutrally than you do in your personal life. To that end, it's important not to come across as antagonistic, accusatory, or egotistical in a work environment. Instead of reinforcing the office hierarchy by reminding people of your position or putting anyone down to make yourself look better, remember that any of these people could one day be your boss. It's always wise to stay out of gossip and not provide fodder for any gossip about yourself by doing your job with direct, effective communication and respect.

*Don't Say:*

"Who's this?"

"Who's calling?"

*Say:*

"Can I help you?"

"Whom may I say is calling?"

*Don't Say:*

"What is this about?"

*Say:*

"What is this regarding?"

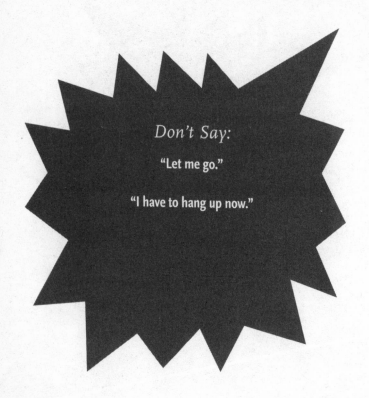

Don't Say:

"Let me go."

"I have to hang up now."

*Say:*

"I'll let you go."

"I know you've got to go."

Don't Say:

"Work for"

Say:

"Work with"

*Don't Say:*

"You've had your chance."

*Say:*

"You've been given plenty
of opportunities."

*Don't Say:*

"That's not the way we do things."

*Say:*

"That's not our usual procedure."

*Don't Say:*

**"Stop being so critical."**

*Say:*

"I feel like I'm being attacked."

*Don't Say:*

"You're the only one who . . ."

*Say:*

"I don't mean to single you out . . ."

Don't Say:

"Let me give you a piece of advice."

Say:

"Here's something that might be helpful."

*Don't Say:*

**"Here's what you need to do . . ."**

*Say:*

"Here's what I would suggest . . ."

"You might want to consider . . ."

*Don't Say:*

"Could you give me some help here?"

*Say:*

"I'd appreciate your support."

**Don't Say:**

"I've got a bone to pick with you."

**Say:**

"May I have a word with you privately?"

# Things Shrinks Say

Psychiatrists and psychologists will tell you that a great deal of their training is focused on not saying anything that might alienate patients or prevent them from opening up. Rather than saying something like, "Tell me what's wrong," they will say, "How are you feeling?"

Similarly, rather than saying to a patient, "I think your problem may be . . . ," they will say, "It seems to me . . . ," or "I wonder if . . ."

These three phrases—"How are you feeling?" "It seems to me . . . ," and "I wonder if . . ."—work just as well when used by real people in real-life situations.

3/2/12

2/10

1/20/12

9
3 x